First Published 2021 by
Redback Publishing
PO Box 357 Frenchs Forest NSW 2086
Australia

www.redbackpublishing.com
orders@redbackpublishing.com

© Redback Publishing 2021

ISBN 978-1-922322-48-7

All rights reserved. No part of this publication may be reproduced in anyform or by any means (including photocopying or storing it in any medium by electronic means and whether or not transiently or incidentally to some other use of this publication) without the written permission of the copyright owner. Applications for the copyright owner's written permission should be addressed to the publisher.

Author: Jane Hinchey
Editor: Marlene Vaughan
Design: Redback Publishing

Original illustrations © Redback Publishing 2021
Originated by Redback Publishing

Printed and bound in China
Acknowledgements

Abbreviations: l—left, r—right, b—bottom, t—top, c—centre, m—middle
We would like to thank the following for permission to reproduce photographs: (Images © shutterstock) p7br Attila JANDI, p8br beeboys, p13br Sean Pavone, p14tl Aleksandar Todorovic, p15mr Aleksandar Todorovic, p18ml Dan Thornberg, p19br Serkant Hekimci, p21tl Juan Salmoral Franco, p21tr yukihipo, p21ml julianne.hide, p21bl Shawn. ccf, p21br kqlsm, p22br icemanphotos, p25tr Club4traveler, p25ml Sean Pavone, p27l Sean Pavone, p28l Osaze Cuomo, p29bl Kobby Dagan, p30mr Benny Marty, p30bl EvergreenPlanet, p31br NCSchneider_Images.

Every effort has been made to contact copyright holders of any material reproduced in this book. Any omissions will be rectified in subsequent printings if notice is given to the publisher.

Disclaimer
All the internet addresses (URLs) given in this book were valid at the time of going to press. However, due to the dynamic nature of the internet, some addresses may have changed, or sites may have changed or ceased to exist since publication. While the author and publisher regret any inconvenience this may cause readers, no responsibility for any such changes can be accepted by either the author or the publisher.

A catalogue record for this book is available from the National Library of Australia

MIX
Paper from responsible sources
FSC® C020056

CONTENTS

Map of Japan 4
Welcome to Japan 6
The Imperial Throne 7
People 8
Daily Life 10
Work 11
Education 12
Clothing 13
Language 14
Life in Cities 15
Life in Rural Areas 16
The Samurai 17
Hiroshima 18
Religion 19
Food 22
Landscape and Climate 24
Important Sites 26
The Arts 28
The Bullet Train 30
Flags, Symbols and Emblems 31
Glossary 32
Index 32

MAP OF JAPAN

MONGOLIA

CHINA

Imperial Palace
TOKYO

Kinkaku-ji
KYOTO

cityscape
KYOTO

SNAPSHOT

COUNTRY Japan

CAPITAL Tokyo

OFFICIAL LANGUAGE Japanese

AREA 377,973 square kilometres

POPULATION 126,000,000 (2020)

RELIGIONS Buddhism, Shintoism

CURRENCY ¥ Yen

Hiroshima
MIYAJIMA ISLAND

Nagasaki
JAPAN

Okinawa
JAPAN

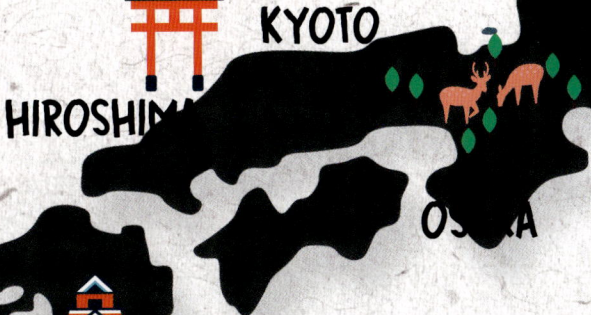

Japan

Mount Fuji
LAKE KAWAGUCHIKO

WELCOME TO JAPAN

When you think of Japan, do you think of sushi and samurai and sakura (cherry blossoms)? Japan is famous for all these, but is also a country with so much more.

Japan is located off the coast of mainland Asia. It consists of four main islands and approximately 6,000 smaller islands, some tiny. About 450 of these islands are inhabited. Most Japanese people live on Honshu, the largest island.

Japan is a democratic, constitutional monarchy. It has a parliamentary government headed by a Prime Minister. It also has an Imperial family, headed by the Emperor.

Japanese people value manners and have certain rules of etiquette around the home:

› Never wear shoes in the house. They must be removed at the front door. Most homes provide slippers for guests.

› Never wash with soap in a bath. A bathtub is for soaking. Wash in the shower and then soak in the tub.

› When visiting a Japanese home, take a gift. Your host will give you a gift back, and you'll need to follow that up with another gift, a process which can continue for some time.

THE IMPERIAL THRONE

Akihito was Japan's 125th Emperor. His family dynasty is the longest running monarchy in the world. During his reign there was much concern in Japan for the future of the Imperial family. In June 2017, a law was passed that allowed the 83 year old Akihito to abdicate due to his advanced age. On April 30, 2019, Emperor Akihito abdicated, making him the first Japanese Emperor to do so in over two centuries. This paved the way for Crown Prince Naruhito to rise to the Imperial Throne.

Crown Prince Naruhito - the Emperor is never referred to by his given name. He is referred to as "His Majesty the Emperor"

Emperor Akihito's reign was from 1989 to 2019

Naruhito has one daughter, but princesses are excluded from succession. Naruhito's brother had a son in 2006. He is Prince Hisahito and is the first male heir born to the Imperial family since 1965. He is now heir to the Imperial Throne.

PEOPLE

Japan has a population of over 126 million people, which is the eleventh largest population in the world. Over 99 per cent of Japan's population is Japanese.

Origins

Hunter-gatherers called Jomon flourished between 10,500 BC and 300 BC. Immigrants from mainland Asia started arriving around 400 BC. The Yayoi, from China, brought rice and settled the lowlands. Present-day Japanese are descendants of the Yayoi people.

The Ainu

Japan's indigenous people are the Ainu. They are ethnically distinct from other Japanese people, and have their own language, religion and culture. About 25,000 Ainu live in Japan today, mostly on the northern island of Hokkaido.

Yoshinogari Historical Park
KANZAKI, JAPAN

An Ageing Population

Japan's population is ageing faster than any other country in the world. The country has a high life-expectancy and a falling birth rate. This is placing great economic strain on the healthcare system. Traditionally, families look after their ageing relatives, but family dynamics have changed over the past few decades, and aged care has become big business in Japan.

DAILY LIFE

Family is important in Japan, but multi-generational homes are not as common as they once were. Families now share small apartments, and children often live at home until they marry. While the home is still the domain of the women, this too is changing, with more women choosing careers outside the home.

A Japanese person's life is filled with many responsibilities and traditions, from birth until death. Behaviour, honesty and manners are important.

Japanese people show respect to others by bowing.

WORK

Japanese carp kites on 5 May for Children's Day
JAPAN

Some Japanese work up to 80 hours a week
TOKYO FINANCIAL DISTRICT

Work is very important to Japanese people. Nearly 70 per cent of employees are company workers in business and big corporations. The working week is 44 hours, although many people work more than that. The Japanese rarely take holidays, although there are numerous public holidays throughout the year.

How to Relax!

Japanese people work and study hard, but they also like to enjoy themselves. Japan's cities come alive after work with people dining out, drinking, and singing in karaoke bars. Japanese people like to study, and often enrol in language classes or courses to learn hobbies. They enjoy watching sports such as baseball, football and the national sport, sumo wrestling.

EDUCATION

Children in Japan are expected to work hard at school. Most children attend public schools, which are free. All children attend six years of elementary school, followed by three years in high school. After that, students who pass their exams may continue to study for another three years. Classes run from Monday to Friday, although some schools have Saturday classes. Many children attend after-school 'cram lessons', and English classes are also popular. The schooling system is based on the American system and was introduced after the Second World War.

CLOTHING

The kimono is the traditional dress of Japan. Kimonos are generally made of silk, with large sleeves, and are tied with a wide belt called an 'obi'. Kimonos are now worn only on special occasions, although some women still wear them for work, festivals or for traditional hobbies. In summer, a 'yukata', or lightweight kimono, is sometimes worn by children and young adults at festivals and other special occasions.

Japanese people wear western clothes now, while some young Japanese take street fashion to an extreme. In the Tokyo suburb of Harajuku there are many different fashion 'tribes'.

LANGUAGE

Japan has one official language: Japanese. Standard Japanese is generally considered to be the language you hear and speak in Tokyo, but there are many different dialects.

Written Japanese is complicated. Japan has several writing systems.
- Kanji
- Hiragana
- Katakana
- Romaji

調和 Harmony

Dream

道 Way

人 Human

日本 Japan

幸 Happiness

One life, one meeting

愛 Love

LIFE IN CITIES

Over 90 per cent of Japan's population lives in cities and nearby suburbs. Half of the population lives in the three major cities of Tokyo, Osaka and Nagoya.

The largest city is Tokyo with a population of almost 14 million people. Over 38 million people live in the greater Tokyo area. Tokyo is actually 26 cities all rolled into one, each with its own unique feel. Within each neighbourhood, there is a strong sense of community.

People who live in the cities often travel long distances on packed trains to get to work. The peak hour trains are famous for being crowded and some stations employ conductors to push people into carriages during peak hours, so the doors can close.

Traditionally, people live in homes made of wood, but concrete houses and apartments are now more common. Most homes have at least one traditional room, with floor mats made from tatami straw. Many families roll the bedding out each night and put it away each morning. This way people can make use of the space during the day.

LIFE IN RURAL AREAS

Japan is a mountainous country. Rural communities struggle with ageing and shrinking populations as young people move to the cities. For those who stay, their way of life has not changed much for generations. Families still live in traditional style homes and own smaller farms and plots of land. Most farms are less than two hectares and produce more than one crop a year. Rice is the main crop, but farmers also grow other cereals, vegetables and fruit.

Along the coast and on islands, millions of people make a living from fishing. About 30 per cent of all fresh fish consumed in the world is eaten by the Japanese.

Homes in rural areas are larger than in cities, and usually built in the traditional style, with sliding wood and rice paper doors and windows. People sit on cushions around the dinner table and sleep on futons on the floor.

THE SAMURAI

The samurai, or shogun, were members of the military caste. They rose to power in the 12th century, and dominated government and society. Imperial rule was restored during the Meiji Restoration of 1868.

Meiji Shrine is the Shinto shrine that is dedicated to the deified spirits of Emperor Meiji and his wife, Empress Shoken.

HIROSHIMA

On August 6, 1945 at 8.16 am, an American B-29 bomber, the Enola Gay, flew over Hiroshima and dropped the world's first atom bomb. It killed 80,000 people and injured 35,000. By the end of the year, another 60,000 people had died.

Mushroom cloud of the atom bomb
NAGASAKI, JAPAN IN 1945

Another bomb was dropped on Nagasaki three days later. Two weeks later, Emperor Hirohito issued a decree ordering all Japanese forces to demobilise and cease operations. This ended the Second World War.

Today

Hiroshima is a modern city with much to see and do, yet many people visit to reflect on the city's past. Visitors to Hiroshima visit the Peace Park and Memorial Museum, which commemorates the bombing and helps to educate visitors on the dangers of nuclear armaments.

RELIGION

Japan's two major religions are Shinto and Buddhism, and most Japanese practise a mix of both. Many homes contain family Shinto shrines and Buddhist altars.

Shinto

There are around 100,000 Shinto shrines in Japan. Shinto means 'Way of the Gods'. It is the indigenous religion of Japan and dates back to prehistoric times. There is no known founder of Shintoism or writer of its sacred texts. In Shintoism, spirits called 'kami' inhabit everything. All animals, plants and natural phenomena contain a divine spirit.

Buddhism

Buddhism is practised by most Japanese in one form or another. There are six major schools of Buddhism in Japan.

Pagodas are multistoried towers with roofs that curve up into sharp, pointed ends

Is it a Shrine or a Temple?

Shintoism is practised at a shrine while Buddhism is practised at a temple. But how can you tell the difference?

> You always enter a Shinto shrine through a 'torii' gate, while a Buddhist temple often contains a pagoda.

> Shinto shrines use the suffix 'jingu', while Buddhist temples use the suffix 'ji' in their names.

> There is often a pair of guardian dogs or lions at the entrance to a Shinto shrine, while a Buddhist temple always houses an image of the Buddha.

> A Shinto shrine contains a purification fountain, while a Buddhist temple contains a large incense burner.

Tea Ceremony

Tea is very much a part of daily life in Japan and has been around for hundreds of years. 'Matcha' green tea is so important that a whole ceremony has been developed around its use. The Japanese tea ceremony, also known as Way of Tea, has its roots in Zen Buddhism. What began as a form of meditation is now an important cultural tradition and is often performed for tourists.

Kodomo no Hi is Japan's annual children's festival on 5 May

Sanja Matsuri in May
TOKYO'S ASAKUSA SHRINE

Awa Odori is the largest traditional dance festival in Japan

Five Fun Festivals!

Japanese people celebrate thousands of festivals each year. Here are five favourites

The Nebuta Matsuri features floats with huge lanterns, and draws crowds of several million people annually

Gion Festival goes on for a month
TOKYO

FOOD

Japan's staple dish is rice, and it is even eaten for breakfast. In Japan, a traditional breakfast consists of rice, miso soup, pickled vegetables and fish. Lunch is similar.

School children either eat a hot lunch provided by their school, or they take a carefully prepared 'bento' (lunch) box from home. A bento box will contain a number of foods in separate sections. Dinner is usually an array of dishes placed in the centre of the table and shared, with people using chopsticks.

Japanese people enjoy eating out. Restaurants often specialise in one specific type of dish, so customers go to a particular place to eat dishes such as ramen, shabu-shabu or okonomiyaki. In sukiyaki restaurants the customers' food is cooked at their table.

ON THE MENU

Sukiyaki

thinly sliced beef cooked with vegetables, seasoned with soy sauce and mirin

Sashimi

sliced raw fish, seasoned with soy sauce and wasabi

Tempura

battered, deep friend vegetables and seafood

Yakitori

skewers of grilled chicken, beef, seafood and vegetables

Noodles

udon and soba noodles are eaten in various ways, both hot and cold

Miso soup

a fermented soybean soup that is another staple in the Japanese diet

LANDSCAPE AND CLIMATE

Japan is a small country located off the coast of mainland Asia. It consists of four main islands and approximately 6,000 smaller islands. About 450 of these islands are inhabited. It is located on the Ring of Fire and sits in one of the most unstable areas of the world. It experiences regular earthquakes and volcanic eruptions.

Ring of Fire on Pacific earthquake belt

Nearly 80 per cent of Japan is mountainous and each of the four main islands has a mountainous central region. It has 10 per cent of the world's volcanoes, including Mount Fuji, which last erupted in the 1700s but is still considered active.

Did You Know?

Japan has about 1,500 earthquakes a year, more than anywhere else on earth.

Although Japan's lowlands are home to sprawling cities and towns, the country still has stunning scenery, from the Japan Alps to dramatic coastlines; from the spruce and fir forests of Hokkaido and Shikoku to the subtropical islands and coral reefs around Okinawa.

Mount Fuji

This iconic mountain is 3,776 metres above sea level, and is Japan's tallest mountain. It is believed to be sacred and appears in myths and legends as well as famous artworks and in literature. Each year over 300,000 people climb Mount Fuji. For the less adventurous, there are numerous well-known viewing spots

Red Fuji by Japanese artist, Hokusai

Climate

Japan's climate varies greatly, depending on the terrain, but generally the country has four distinct seasons. In the mountainous north, freezing winds can sweep in from Siberia. The Japan Alps are famous for their ski fields. Summer on the coast is hot and humid, and a rainy season occurs in June. During the warmer months, typhoons are common and account for about a third of the country's annual rainfall. Spring is from March to May. During this time the country's cherry blossom trees are in full bloom and Japanese people celebrate with festivals and cherry blossom viewing parties.

Hot Springs

The onsen is an important part of Japanese culture, and bathing in them can be ritualistic. There are over 3,000 to choose from, with different therapeutic benefits and etiquette rules to follow.

IMPORTANT SITES

Japan is home to many of the world's most famous and important historical sites. Over 31 million people visit Japan annually, often to see these incredible places.

Kamakura Buddha

This bronze statue of Buddha, which dates from 1252, is 13.35 metres high and weighs 93 tonnes. It was originally housed in a temple but that was washed away by a huge tsunami in the late 1400s.

Kyoto

The ancient capital of Kyoto served as the Emperor's residence from 794 to 1868. There are over 1,600 temples and 400 shrines in Kyoto. Due to its historic value it was spared bombing during the Second World War. Visitors now flock to see its many famous sites, including the Kiyomizudera and Kinkaku-ji (golden) temples, and the Sagano Bamboo Forest. The historic district of Gion is the birthplace of the geisha, and visitors to Kyoto are sometimes lucky enough to spot a geisha on her way to work.

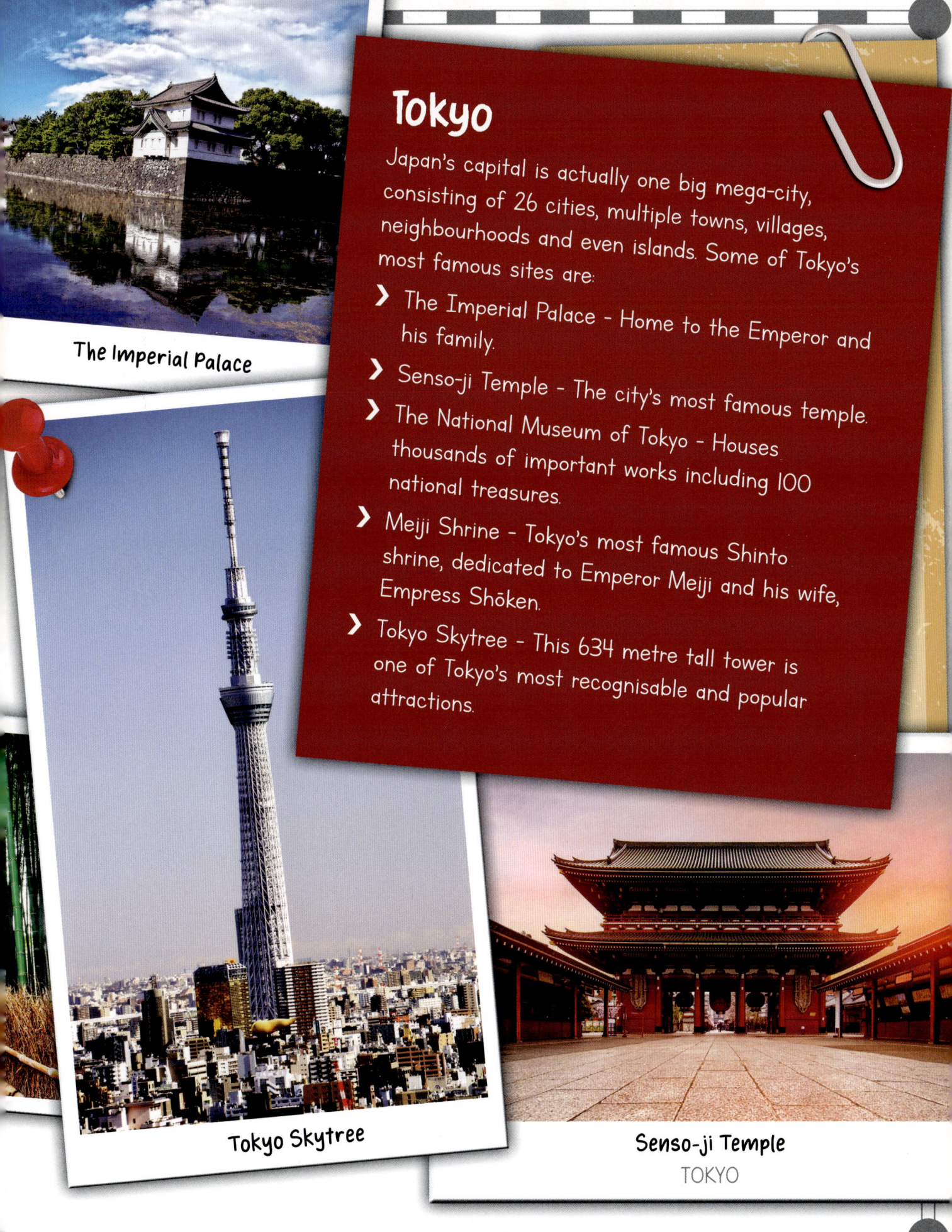

The Imperial Palace

Tokyo

Japan's capital is actually one big mega-city, consisting of 26 cities, multiple towns, villages, neighbourhoods and even islands. Some of Tokyo's most famous sites are:

› The Imperial Palace - Home to the Emperor and his family.

› Senso-ji Temple - The city's most famous temple.

› The National Museum of Tokyo - Houses thousands of important works including 100 national treasures.

› Meiji Shrine - Tokyo's most famous Shinto shrine, dedicated to Emperor Meiji and his wife, Empress Shōken.

› Tokyo Skytree - This 634 metre tall tower is one of Tokyo's most recognisable and popular attractions.

Tokyo Skytree

Senso-ji Temple
TOKYO

THE ARTS

Japan's traditional arts were strongly influenced by China, but over centuries they made these arts their own. Modern arts such as cinema, manga (comics) and music styles are often unique to Japan and celebrated all over the world.

Watch

Film director, animator and manga artist, Hayao Miyazaki has produced some incredible films, including:

- Kiki's Delivery Service
- Spirited Away
- My Neighbor Totoro
- Howl's Moving Castle
- Princess Mononoke

Music

Traditional music is divided into three categories: theatrical, court music and instrumental. A range of string, wind and percussion instruments is used in traditional music. One of the most famous is the shamisen, a banjo-like lute with three strings. Today, many styles of music are popular, but pop music 'rules', especially Japan's own J-pop. Karaoke is hugely popular as well.

Japanese Calligraphy

Decorative handwriting is considered a great art in Japan. Each kanji character is written with strokes in a certain order. Children often attend classes to learn the art of 'shodo', or the 'Way of Writing'.

The Performing Arts

Many of Japan's performing arts traditions are centuries old, but continue to be popular today, and none more so than kabuki. This colourful theatre form dates back to the 1600s. It is performed by men in colourful costumes with an exaggerated style, accompanied by instruments, clappers and chanting. The average length of a performance is five hours, however audience members come and go, and eat and drink during the play.

Origami

The art of paper folding has been practised in Japan since the Edo period (1603-1867) and was both ceremonial and recreational. Japanese children continue to learn origami today.

THE BULLET TRAIN

Japan has one of the most sophisticated transport systems in the world. Modern transport systems move people and goods all around the country. Public transport is efficient and the preferred mode of transport for many people.

Japanese trains are some of the most efficient, punctual and safe in the world. Over 100 private companies provide railway services, and the major cities have both above ground and subway lines.

Japan's most famous mode of transport is the shinkansen, or bullet train. The first railway line was opened in 1872, but it was in the early sixties that the extensive bullet train system was first developed during preparations for the 1964 Tokyo Olympics. With the success of the shinkansen, Japan became a world leader in fast trains. Today the shinkansen has a top operational commercial speed of 320 kilometres per hour.

FLAGS SYMBOLS AND EMBLEMS

Flag of Japan

The national flag consists of one crimson disc on a white background. The flag is officially called 'Nishokki', meaning 'sun mark' flag, but is more commonly known as 'Hinomaru', meaning 'circle of the sun'. The red circle does represent the sun, but in Japan the Emperor is also known as the 'son of the sun'. While the flag has been used for over a thousand years, it was officially adopted as the flag of Imperial Japan on January 27, 1870.

National Animal

Japan's national animal is the carp.

National Flower

There is no official national flower in Japan, but the cherry blossom and the chrysanthemum are both considered special. The cherry blossom is the national tree, while the chrysanthemum is the Imperial Seal.

Imperial Seal

The Imperial Seal of Japan is also called the 'Chrysanthemum Seal'. The chrysanthemum is a symbol of the Emperor and his family. The central disc of this yellow emblem is surrounded by sixteen petals.

GLOSSARY

Buddhism	religion based on the teachings of Buddha
culture	practices, beliefs and customs of a society or people
endangered	when a species is at risk
ethnic group	people who share a common culture, language and heritage
highlands	mountainous or elevated region
monsoon	season of heavy rain
plateau	large, flat area found in higher regions
sustainability	supporting the environment
tatami mats	woven mats, traditionally made of rice straw

INDEX

arts 28, 29
Buddhism 4, 19, 20, 32
climate 24, 25
clothing 13
daily life 10, 15, 16, 20
education 12
flag 31
food 22, 23
geisha 26
Hiroshima 5, 18
Imperial throne 7
landscape 24
language 4, 8, 11, 14
map 4
religion 4, 8, 19, 32
samurai 6, 17
Shintoism 4, 17, 19, 20, 27
Tokyo 4, 5, 11, 13,-15, 21, 27, 30
work 11, 13, 15, 26